GREAT MINDS OF SCIENCE

ISAAC NEWTON

Genius Mathematician and Physicist

by Carla Mooney

Content Consultant
Dr. Katherine Brading
Associate Professor of Philosophy
University of Notre Dame

Core Library

An Imprint of Abdo Publishing
www.abdopublishing.com

www.abdopublishing.com

Published by Abdo Publishing, a division of ABDO, PO Box 398166, Minneapolis, Minnesota 55439. Copyright © 2015 by Abdo Consulting Group, Inc. International copyrights reserved in all countries. No part of this book may be reproduced in any form without written permission from the publisher. Core Library™ is a trademark and logo of Abdo Publishing.

Printed in the United States of America, North Mankato, Minnesota
042014
092014

THIS BOOK CONTAINS
RECYCLED MATERIALS

Cover Photo: Georgios Kollidas/Shutterstock Images
Interior Photos: Georgios Kollidas/Shutterstock Images, 1; Thinkstock, 4; Justus Sustermans, 7; Robert Cutts, 9; Awe Inspiring Images/Shutterstock Images, 10; Vasilieva Tatiana/Shutterstock Images, 12; Bettmann/Corbis, 14; Heritage Images/Corbis, 17; Shutterstock Images, 20, 45; Jim Sugar/Corbis, 22, 43; The Print Collector/Corbis, 24; Webspark/Shutterstock Images, 26; Newton/PoodlesRock/PoodlesRock/Corbis, 28; Borsvelka/Shutterstock Images, 32 (top); Sarininka/Shutterstock Images, 32 (bottom); Klaus-Dieter Keller, 34; Library of Congress, 36; Pete Spiro/Shutterstock Images, 41

Editor: Jenna Gleisner
Series Designer: Becky Daum

Library of Congress Control Number: 2014932619

Cataloging-in-Publication Data
Mooney, Carla.
 Isaac Newton: genius mathematician and physicist / Carla Mooney.
   p. cm. -- (Great minds of science)
Includes bibliographical references and index.
ISBN 978-1-62403-382-7
1. Newton, Isaac, 1642-1727--Juvenile literature. 2. Physicists--Great Britain--Biography--Juvenile literature. 3. Mathematicians--Great Britain--Biography--Juvenile literature. I. Title.
530.092--dc23
[B]
                                              2014932619

CONTENTS

CHAPTER ONE

EARLY LIFE

Isaac Newton has been called the greatest scientist who ever lived. He introduced the laws of motion and developed the theory of gravity. Along with modern philosophers of the time, such as Galileo Galilei and Johannes Kepler, Newton changed the way we learn about science today. He paved the way for scientists who would come after him. He showed scientists how to explore and test the world

Isaac Newton is often honored as the most influential mathematician and scientist of all time.

around them. But before becoming famous, Isaac Newton lived a very ordinary life.

Ordinary Childhood

Isaac Newton was born on Christmas Day, 1642, at Woolsthorpe Manor in Lincolnshire, England. His mother, Hannah Ayscough Newton, named him Isaac after his father. Isaac's father had died a few months before Isaac's birth. When Isaac was three years old, his mother married a clergyman named Barnabas Smith. She went to live with her new husband in the nearby village of North

Galileo Galilei

Galileo Galilei was a scientist and astronomer. He was born in 1564 near Pisa, Italy. Galileo experimented with motion and how objects fall to Earth. He proved that all objects fall at the same rate of acceleration, whether they are heavy or light. Galileo also built a telescope to study the moon, planets, and stars. At the time, many people believed that the sun orbited Earth. Galileo disagreed. He supported the theory of Polish astronomer Nicolaus Copernicus, which stated that Earth circled the sun. Newton studied Galileo's work on motion and gravity.

Galileo's experiments and theories set in motion scientists' ideas about gravity.

Witham. Young Isaac stayed behind at Woolsthorpe Manor. His grandmother cared for him. Daily life in Isaac's village was simple. He attended classes in nearby villages. There he learned to read, write, and count. He attended church services every Sunday.

Johannes Kepler

Before Newton was born, other scientists were laying the groundwork for his future studies. One of the most influential was Johannes Kepler. Kepler was a German astronomer who lived from 1571 to 1630. He studied the way the planets move. He believed that the planets orbit the sun instead of the earth. He discovered that the planets do not orbit the sun in a perfect circle. Instead, their path is in the shape of an ellipse, a figure that looks like a circle that has been stretched in one direction. Kepler was the first scientist to find a simple mathematical rule to describe how planets speed up and slow down as they orbit.

The King's School

In 1653 Barnabas Smith died. Isaac's mother returned to Woolsthorpe Manor when Isaac was 10 years old. His mother brought along three young children from her marriage to Smith. A year or two later, Isaac was sent to the King's School. This was a school for boys in Grantham, England. It was too far to travel each day, so Isaac lived with the Clark family. William Clark was the town's apothecary. An apothecary was similar to

Newton learned Latin, some Greek and Hebrew, and arithmetic at the King's School in Grantham, England.

Newton's home, Woolsthorpe Manor, still stands in Lincolnshire, England.

a pharmacist. He mixed potions, powders, ointments, and herbal remedies. It is possible that Isaac became interested in science while staying with the Clarks.

At the King's School, Isaac was expected to learn by memorizing what he read. Isaac thought many of his lessons were boring. He liked to read books from the library and study machines instead. He built models of windmills, mousetraps, and other gadgets.

In 1658, when Isaac was 16 years old, his mother pulled him out of school. She wanted him to learn how to farm so that he could run Woolsthorpe Manor.

But Isaac thought farming was incredibly boring. He let his pigs and sheep wander. His fences needed repair. He was a miserable farmer. Finally Isaac's uncle, William, and his schoolmaster talked to his mother. They convinced her to let Isaac go back to school. He returned to the King's School to finish his basic studies.

FURTHER EVIDENCE

There is a lot of information about Isaac Newton's early years in Chapter One. If you could pick out the main point of the chapter, what would it be? Find a few pieces of key evidence from the chapter that support the main point. Then explore the website below to learn even more about Newton's early years. Find a quote from the website that supports the chapter's main point. Does the quote support an existing piece of evidence in the chapter? Or does it add a new piece of evidence? Why?

Isaac Newton

www.mycorelibrary.com/isaac-newton

CHAPTER TWO

STUDYING AT CAMBRIDGE

In 1661 Newton enrolled in Trinity College at Cambridge University in London, England. At first he studied Greek, Latin, and Hebrew languages. He also studied ancient Greek philosophers. The ideas of the ancient Greeks had been accepted for 2,000 years. Newton worked hard, but he became interested in modern science. He spent most of his time reading works from modern philosophers,

While studying at the Trinity College at Cambridge, Newton became interested in philosophy and science.

Probl I

Investiganda est curva Linea ADB in qua grave a dato quovis puncto A ad datum quodvis punctum B vi gravitatis suæ citissimè descendet

Solutio.

A dato puncto A ducatur recta infinita APCZ horizonti parallela et super eadem recta describatur tum Cyclois quæcunqus AQP recta (recta et si opus est producta) occurrens in puncto Q, tum Cyclois alia ADC cujus basis et altitudo sit ad prioris basem et altitudinem respectivè ut AB ad AQ. Et hæc Cyclois novissima transibit per punctum B et erit Curva illa linea in qua grave a puncto A ad punctum B vi gravitatis suæ citissimè pervraiet. Q. E. I

such as Galileo Galilei, Johannes Kepler, and René Descartes. The modern philosophers challenged the ideas the ancient Greeks had about science. Newton was determined to find out if the ancient philosophers or modern philosophers were correct.

Experimenting as a Scientist

Newton began keeping a scientific notebook. He called it *Quaestiones Quaedam Philosophicae* (Certain Philosophical Questions). He filled the notebook with topics he wanted to research. His topics included questions about time, space, motion, stars, light, vision, and colors. He set up experiments in his room and carefully recorded his observations. Newton was now a scientist.

Newton had little money to buy equipment. So he tested his experiments on himself. For example, he used his own eyes to test how vision and colors can change in different lighting. One day at sunset, he took a dark feather and put it in front of his eyes. He observed the colors around the feather's edge. He described all of his observations about vision in his notes.

Dangerous Experiments

Some of the experiments Newton conducted on himself could be very dangerous. During one experiment, he pushed a needle behind his eyeball to see how it changed his vision. Yet another time he stared directly into the sun to see how it affected his vision. Afterward he had to spend several days in a dark room until his vision returned to normal.

Moving Back Home

In January 1665, Newton received his bachelor's degree from Cambridge. He was also awarded a scholarship. The scholarship would help pay for even more education. Newton planned to stay at Cambridge and continue his research. The Great Plague had struck London in late 1664. The plague was a highly contagious and deadly disease that continued to spread in 1665. It killed thousands of people. As the plague spread, people panicked and fled the city. Cambridge University

The Great Plague

The bubonic plague, also called the Great Plague, struck London in late 1664. It began to spread throughout the city in 1665. At the time, people did not know that it was spread by fleas from rats to humans. People who were infected experienced fevers and aches. They soon developed black swellings in their armpits. Within days most infected people died. Many people fled London to live in the countryside, away from other people. By September 1665, the plague was killing 8,000 people each week.

Mass graves were dug for the 75,000 to 100,000 people the Great Plague killed.

closed. Newton left London and returned home to Woolsthorpe Manor. But he continued his studies.

Back at home, Newton set up a study in his bedroom. Without schoolwork, he was able to think about ideas that fascinated him. He set up new

17

experiments to test. One of Newton's interests was mathematics. He invented a system to calculate how things change over time. Newton called his method fluxions. Today it is known as calculus. It was an important tool Newton would use in his future work.

While home at Woolsthorpe, Newton also thought about gravity. He read one of Galileo's books. The book described how objects fall to Earth. Newton had already studied the writings of German astronomer Johannes Kepler and thought about how planets move in orbit. He thought that the force that brings objects to Earth might be the same force that causes the moon to circle Earth.

In 1667 Cambridge University reopened and Newton returned to London. His time at Woolsthorpe had been worthwhile. With no interruptions and no distractions, Newton had done some of his most brilliant thinking. He laid the foundation for his future work in mathematics, optics, and motion.

Newton writes about his observations of freezing and thawing in his notebook passage titled "Of Heate & Cold":

> Apples, Eggs, Cheeses, Men. . . . frozen are vitiated by freezing but not soe much when thawed by water or snow as by fire. Frost will breake stones, crack trees, make the Humor chrystall looke white.
>
> A man cannot feele where hee is frozen & though frozen all over feeles onely a prickling in his recovery, hee may bee recovered being dipped in water or rubbed over with snow, but not by a Stove. Nay any frozen part is lost which is thawed in a Stove. & the fier pains us in warming our cold fingers. Frozen meate layd to thaw & roast by the fire will bee raw in the midst after many Howers.
>
> Though frost change & destroy bodys (espetialy in the thawing) yet cold preserves them.
>
> Source: Isaac Newton. "Quæstiones quædam Philosophiæ." The Newton Project. Cambridge University Library, n.d. Web. Accessed February 5, 2014.

Consider Your Audience

Review this passage closely. Consider how you would rewrite it for a different audience, such as your parents, principal, or friends. Write a blog post conveying this same information for the new audience. Write it so that they can understand it. How is your version different from the original text, and why?

CHAPTER THREE

LIGHT AND COLORS

Newton received his master of arts degree from Cambridge University in 1669. Around this time he wrote an essay that explained his theories of calculus. He shared this paper with Isaac Barrow, the mathematics professor at Cambridge. Barrow was impressed with Newton's work. When Barrow retired, Newton was offered

Newton became Cambridge University's mathematics professor in 1669.

The mirror in Newton's telescope made images look much sharper than did earlier telescopes, which used lenses.

Barrow's job as Cambridge University's mathematics professor.

A New Telescope

One of the first topics Newton worked on and taught about was optics. Newton had begun his work with optics when he first arrived at Cambridge. In his research, he had used telescopes that were already created. These telescopes used lenses, which often created an image that was hard to see. For years, people had tried to create a better telescope.

Newton had built his own telescope in 1668. His telescope used a mirror instead of a lens. It made objects appear 40 times larger than their real size. In 1671 Newton sent his telescope to the Royal Society in London. The Royal Society appreciated his scientific work and made Newton a member in 1672.

The Royal Society

In the mid-1640s, a group of philosophers began meeting in London to discuss their ideas about science. In 1660 a group of 12 men met at Gresham College in London. They founded the Royal Society. The society met regularly to conduct experiments and talk about science. Members believed research and experiments must be conducted to prove a theory.

Prisms and Light

Newton was also fascinated by light. At a local fair, he bought a glass triangle called a prism. When light passes through a prism, it comes out as bands of color. Most people at the time believed that the

Newton experimenting with a prism and light

prism created the bands of color. Newton believed that white light, such as ordinary daylight, contained all of the colors. He conducted several experiments with prisms. He wanted to prove that white light is a mixture of colors. He proved that a prism bends the light. When the light bends, the separate colors of the rainbow become visible.

Praise and Criticism

Newton wrote about his work with prisms and his ideas about light in his first scientific paper. He titled the paper "Theory about Light and Colors." Newton sent his paper to the Royal Society. The Royal Society published Newton's paper in 1672 in their journal. It was well received by many scientists. But a few scientists did not agree with Newton's paper. Robert Hooke, a brilliant scientist and Royal Society member, criticized Newton's work. Hooke had also worked with prisms to study light. He had reached conclusions different from Newton's. Hooke wrote a long paper that criticized Newton's findings.

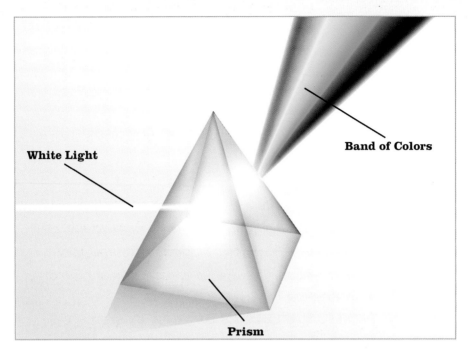

Newton's Prism Experiment

To learn about light, Newton passed a beam of white light through a prism. The prism bent the light and split it into a band of colors resembling the colors of the rainbow: red, orange, yellow, green, blue, indigo, and violet. This diagram shows Newton's prism experiment. How does it support Newton's ideas about the nature of light?

Newton was very angry about Hooke's paper. He even threatened to quit the Royal Society. But he changed his mind when several members urged him to stay. Instead, he wrote a long reply to Hooke's objections. It was the beginning of a lifelong rivalry between the two scientists. Over the years, they would disagree several times over scientific theories.

In this letter to the Royal Society, Newton explains his discovery about light:

> But the most surprising, and wonderful composition was that of Whiteness. There is no one sort of Rays which alone can exhibit this. 'Tis ever compounded, and to its composition are requisite all the aforesaid primary Colours, mixed in a due proportion. I have often with Admiration beheld, that all the Colours of the Prisme being made to converge, and thereby to be again mixed as they were in the light before it was Incident upon the Prisme, reproduced light, intirely and perfectly white, and not at all sensibly differing from a direct Light of the Sun, unless when the glasses, I used, were not sufficiently clear; for then they would a little incline it to their colour.

Source: Isaac Newton. "A Letter of Mr. Isaac Newton . . . Containing His New Theory about Light and Colors." The Newton Project. Cambridge University Library, n.d. Web. Accessed December 13, 2013.

What's the Big Idea?

Reread Newton's letter carefully. Have a parent or teacher help you understand what it means. What is the main idea in the letter? Which details support the main idea? Name two or three details Newton uses to support his main idea.

PHILOSOPHIÆ

NATURALIS

PRINCIPIA

MATHEMATICA.

Autore *JS. NEWTON*, *Trin. Coll. Cantab. Soc.* Matheseos
Professore *Lucasiano*, & Societatis Regalis Sodali.

IMPRIMATUR.
S. PEPYS, *Reg. Soc.* PRÆSES.
Julii 5. 1686.

LONDINI,

Jussu *Societatis Regiæ* ac Typis *Josephi Streater*. Prostat apud
plures Bibliopolas. *Anno* MDCLXXXVII.

WRITING THE GREATEST SCIENCE BOOK

Newton continued to write about his experiments and discoveries. In 1687 he published his most famous work, titled *Philosophiae Naturalis Principia Mathematica* (Mathematical Principles of Natural Philosophy). It was the first book of modern physics that explained how the physical world works. Newton had worked for more than 20 years to perfect his ideas about motion,

Newton's influential book, Principia, was first published in London.

gravity, and the physical world. Today many scientists believe that Newton's *Principia* is one of the most influential books in all of science.

Public Life

After publishing *Principia*, Newton began to take on a more public role. In 1689 he was elected to represent Cambridge in Parliament. In 1696 he was appointed Warden of the Royal Mint. In this role, Newton helped create new coins and even hunted down counterfeiters—people who created and used fake coins. In 1703 he was elected president of the Royal Society. In 1705 Queen Anne of England awarded Newton a great public honor by knighting him, making him Sir Isaac Newton.

Laws of Motion

In *Principia* Newton described what he called the laws of motion. Why and how do objects move? What makes an object stop moving? What happens when an outside force pushes or pulls an object? Newton answered these questions with his three laws of motion.

Newton's first law is called the law of inertia. This law states that an object at rest will stay at rest. It also states that an object in motion will stay in motion in a straight line at a constant speed unless an outside force acts on it.

The second law is called the law of acceleration. This law states that when a force is applied to an object, that object will accelerate. In physics the word *acceleration* is used to describe when an object speeds up, slows down, or changes direction. How much an object accelerates depends on how strong the outside force is. It also depends on the object's mass. Newton introduced the word *mass* to describe

Secret Alchemist

In addition to experimenting with motion, Newton conducted many experiments in alchemy over his lifetime. Alchemy was an early version of chemistry. Most alchemists believed that one element could be changed into another by rearranging its atoms. Alchemists often wanted to turn other metals into gold. Although they were never successful, some useful knowledge about metals and other materials came from their experiments. Critics of alchemy claimed that it was nothing more than a fraud. For the most part, Newton kept his interest in alchemy quiet.

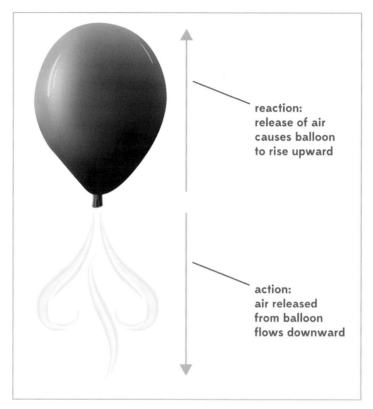

reaction:
release of air
causes balloon
to rise upward

action:
air released
from balloon
flows downward

Newton's Third Law of Motion

Newton's third law of motion states that for every action there is an equal and opposite reaction. Look at the diagram above of a balloon filled with air. When the air is let out, the balloon rises. How does this diagram show the principle of action and reaction? What other everyday objects illustrate Newton's third law of motion?

how much matter there is in an object. An object with greater mass feels heavier than an object with less mass.

Newton's third law of motion is called the law of action and reaction. This law states that every action has an equal and opposite reaction. One way to think about this law is to picture a rocket. Gases from a rocket's burning fuel shoot out the back and push the rocket into the air.

Law of Universal Gravitation

Newton also wrote about his theory of gravity in *Principia*. His law of universal gravitation states that the force of gravity affects all objects, even those beyond Earth. He stated that every object in the universe attracts all other objects. This attraction is the force called gravity. The force of gravitational attraction between two objects depends on the mass of the two objects and the distance between them. Other scientists had similar ideas, but Newton created a mathematical equation to calculate the force. Newton's equation is still used today to estimate the effects of gravity.

Principia made Newton famous around the world. He became one of the most respected scientists in Europe. He spent the remaining years of his life

Millions of tourists visit Newton's grave at Westminster Abbey in London each year.

revising his work. At the end of his life, Newton lived with his niece Catherine Conduitt and her husband near Winchester, England. Although he was famous and wealthy, Newton never married or had many friends.

Fame and Death

As he grew older, Newton's health began to fail. He suffered from a variety of illnesses. In March 1727, Newton died in London at the age of 85. After his death, a funeral was held for him at Westminster Abbey in London. It was a great honor for the scientist. In 1731 a monument to Isaac Newton was placed in Westminster Abbey. It is inscribed in Latin. Part of it reads: "Mortals rejoice that there has existed such and so great an ornament of the human race."

EXPLORE ONLINE

Chapter Four discusses Newton's three laws of motion. The website below further explores Newton's laws of motion. As you know, every source is different. What facts does the website give about Newton's laws of motion? How is the information from the website the same as the information in Chapter Four? What new information did you learn from the website?

Newton's Laws of Motion

www.mycorelibrary.com/isaac-newton

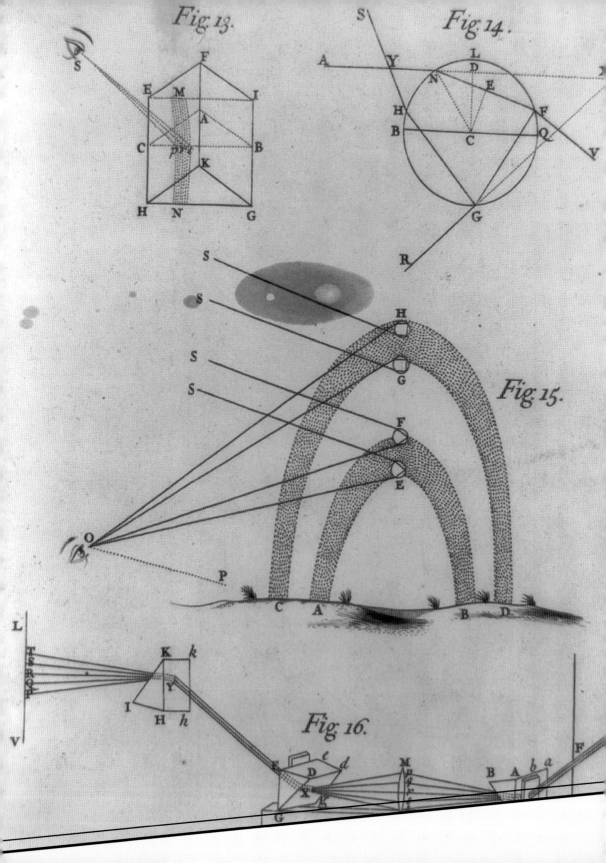

Fig. 13.

Fig. 14.

Fig. 15.

Fig. 16.

CHAPTER FIVE

NEWTON'S IMPACT

Even after his death, Isaac Newton had a lasting impact on the world. His discoveries changed the way people see and understand the universe. Ancient people once thought that unpredictable, supernatural forces controlled the universe. But Newton showed that planets, comets, falling apples, and even ocean tides are predictable using the same set of rules.

Newton's discoveries and methods of research forever changed the study of science.

Scientific Method

Newton is credited with using the scientific method to investigate the world around him. Many scientists use the scientific method to help them learn more about something. The scientific method usually follows the steps below:

1. Make observations.
2. Propose a hypothesis, or an idea that could explain how something will work, to explain the observations.
3. Design and conduct an experiment to test the hypothesis.
4. Study the results of the experiment. Find out if the results support the hypothesis or not.
5. Build on what was learned to develop new tests and hypotheses.

Testing Ideas

Newton also showed how people could investigate and understand the truth about the world around them. He is credited for introducing the scientific method. The scientific method uses experiments and observations to test our ideas and help us learn about the world. Newton inspired the scientists who came after him. Scientists have used the scientific method to make discoveries in chemistry, biology, and every other area of science.

Paving the Way for Sciences

Newton's breakthroughs were the beginning of many scientific discoveries, inventions, and theories. His three laws of motion are the foundation for modern rocket science. Without his work, space travel may never have been possible. Because of the work he did to help understand forces, the unit of measurement for force is named after him. It is called a "newton."

After his death, Newton's fame soared.

Scientific Revolution

Newton was a part of the scientific revolution. The scientific revolution was a period of amazing scientific breakthroughs. It took place around the 1400s, 1500s, and 1600s. During this time, new ideas in physics, astronomy, biology, chemistry, and other sciences emerged. The scientific revolution changed the way people thought about the world around them. Scientists began to question beliefs that had been held since ancient Greece. They carefully observed the world and designed experiments to test their ideas. Other famous scientists, such as Copernicus, Kepler, and Galileo were also part of the scientific revolution.

Science became popular. Average people became interested in science. They gathered to listen to lectures about scientific topics. Groups formed to discuss science. By 1826 the University College London opened. It allowed students to study science as a separate course of study. It trained doctors and engineers. People realized the importance of studying science and how it could be used to improve everyday life and health. Newton's discoveries have lasted for more than 300 years. Newton taught scientists how to question, test, and explain the world around them. His work still guides scientists today.

University College London originally opened as London University, the first university in London.

Scientific Method

Isaac Newton is credited with introducing the scientific method to the world of science. The scientific method is a process of making observations about the world, developing a hypothesis to explain what is observed, testing the hypothesis, and then accepting, rejecting, or changing it for more tests. Newton documented his scientific method in much of his work. Today scientists in every branch of science use the scientific method to question, investigate, and understand the world.

Rocket Science

Newton's laws of motion are the foundation of modern rocket science. They explain how and why rockets work. Newton's laws of motion help scientists understand how rockets work, launch, and fly in space. Newton's laws inspire scientists to experiment with new rocket designs. They use their new understanding of motion to create designs that improve rocket performance and control. Because of Newton, humans are able to walk on the moon and explore deep space.

Reflecting Telescope

Newton designed and built a telescope that uses mirrors instead of lenses. It is called a reflecting telescope. A large mirror captures the image. A smaller mirror reflects it into the viewer's eye. The telescope is much clearer than lens telescopes. It is also much smaller. Today, astronomers use a variation of Newton's telescope design.

Take a Stand

Isaac Newton conducted some very dangerous optics experiments on himself. Do you think experimenting on himself to come to conclusions was a good idea? Write a short essay explaining your opinion. Make sure to give reasons for your opinion, as well as facts and details to support your reasons.

Why Do I Care?

Isaac Newton lived and conducted his scientific experiments hundreds of years ago. But that does not mean his work has not affected your life. Think about two or three ways the life and discoveries of Isaac Newton connect to your own life. Give examples of parts of your life that have a connection to Isaac Newton.

You Are There

Imagine that you live in England in the 1600s. Write 300 words describing your life. What do you see happening in your town? Is your family sick from the Great Plague? How do you go about daily life without modern technology?

Say What?

Find five words in this book that you have never seen or heard before. Find each word in a dictionary and read the definition. Rewrite the word's definition in your own words. Then use each word in a sentence.

GLOSSARY

acceleration
the process of moving faster and faster

arithmetic
a branch of mathematics that deals with numbers and their addition, subtraction, multiplication, and division

calculus
a branch of higher mathematics concerned especially with rates of change and the finding of lengths, areas, and volumes

gravity
the force that pulls objects down toward the surface of the earth and keeps them from floating away into space

inertia
resistance to any change in motion

mass
the amount of matter in an object

optics
a science that deals with the nature and properties of light and the effects that it undergoes and produces

orbit
the invisible path followed by an object circling a planet or the sun

philosopher
a person who seeks knowledge, truth, and wisdom

white light
light that appears colorless but contains all colors of the spectrum

LEARN MORE

Books

Hollihan, Kerrie Logan. *Isaac Newton and Physics for Kids: His Life and Ideas with 21 Activities*. Chicago: Chicago Review Press, 2009.

Krull, Kathleen. *Isaac Newton*. New York: Viking, 2006.

Steele, Phillip. *Isaac Newton: The Scientist Who Changed Everything*. Washington, DC: National Geographic Children's Books, 2013.

Websites

To learn more about Great Minds of Science, visit **booklinks.abdopublishing.com**. These links are routinely monitored and updated to provide the most current information available.

Visit **www.mycorelibrary.com** for free additional tools for teachers and students.

INDEX

ABOUT THE AUTHOR

Carla Mooney is the author of several books for young readers. She loves investigating and learning about people, places, and events in history. She lives in Pittsburgh, Pennsylvania, with her husband and three children.